THE
BE-ATTITUDES
FOR LEADERS

"Attitudes, thoughts, and works of leaders striving for the Kingdom"

PASTOR
ERIKA MCLAURIN

The Be-attitudes for Leaders by Ericka McLaurin © 2017

ISBN-13: 978-0-9998785-0-7

Library of Congress: TXu 2-038-723

Cover: Design by Andrew Ivery ~ andrewlivery@gmail.com

Layout Design by Cynthia Martin-Roper of nVision International ~ www.nVisionInt.com

TABLE OF CONTENTS

DEDICATION

I dedicate this book to the three most important ladies in my life:

Wendy McLaurin
Arielle McLaurin
Paige Kimbrew

You three have been my daily inspiratiosn in this journey.

Acknowledgements

I would like to thank my Lord and Savior, Jesus Christ. Without Him, none of this would be possible. I am extremely grateful for all the strength, wisdom and ability He gave me to complete this book.

I would like to extend my gratitude to several people who have journeyed with me in recent years to complete this book.

I would like to say thank you to my mom Wendy McLaurin. Thank you so much for always wanting the best for me. Your unconditional love, care, concern and trust has made me a stronger person. I can never thank you enough for all your support in this journey.

I would like to say thank you to my two-beautiful daughters Arielle McLaurin, and Paige Kimbrew, for their love, support, and encouragement. You two were my inspiration to keep going until the book was finished.

I would like to say thank you to my dad Thomas McLaurin for showing me how to be a leader.

I would like to say a special thank you for those who read through this manuscript and offered wise advice- Pam Thomas and Lucille Sutton. I appreciate you!

I would like to thank Denise Mayo, Angelique Kelley, Kenya

Campbell, Cherry Rhodes and the sister-cousins for their continual inspiration to finish the book.

I would like to thank Barbara Williams for her continually pushing me beyond any limits I thought I had. Your insight, invaluable comments and friendship has made this possible.

I would also like to thank Pastor Donald Hubbard, Bishop Byron Johnson and Pastor Mark Brown for your encouragement, patience, guidance, expertise and knowledge you have given me as a leader.

Endorsements

"I am pleased to offer my endorsement for such an amazing book. I found it to be. Very helpful in evaluating my leadership skills. I am not a current leader in my church, but I am a leader on my job. This book allowed me to evaluate and adjust the way I lead using kingdom principles. I highly recommend this book to any and all leaders. It will greatly enhance the way and how effectively you lead. I hope there is another installment in the works because teaching like this is greatly needed."

Terra Pearson, MD
Transplant Surgeon and Intensivist
Assistant Professor at the Medical College of Wisconsin

"As a leader in both the church and community, "The Be-Attitudes for Leaders" offers great wisdom and insight on the responsibility of being an effective and integral leader. I encourage you to add to Kingdom work to your arsenal.

Dr. Tuesday Tate, Dr. Th, CHBC, CT, CCLC
Author | Ordained Minister | Motivational Speaker | Certified Trainer and Relationship Coach | Life Advisor | Media Personality | Consultant | Elite and Executive Coach

"Reading this revelatory, Word based book has made a powerful and positive impact on my leadership paradigm already. The thought provoking questions bring a deep level of soul searching that I believe will increase our TRUE usability in service to God. I kept getting the sense that the content presented was so concentrated, and power packed, that it seemed more like a series of training manuals than a devotional. I want to buy this book for our leadership school students, and I want to read it again, and again to activate my own growth. God has placed so much in you Pastor Erika, and as Christian leaders we need the blessing of your life and work. Thank you for this timely offering."

Apostle Gin Burda
Iron Sharpeners Leadership Academy

"I highly recommend Be-Attitudes for Leaders to anyone that desires a fresh Kingdom approach to leadership development. Pastor McLaurin provides an insightful view of Kingdom leadership strategies within the construct of Jesus' teaching of the Beatitudes. Moreover, one will find clarity, depth and balance as she interweaves theological truths with practical life application recommendations. All in all, this is a great book for busy leaders to quickly understand the necessary dynamics for Godly leadership in the 21st century."

Mark V. Brown Sr., Senior Pastor
New Wineskin Ministries, Indianapolis, IN

"Erika has made an epic masterpiece - beautifully aligned with the Bible's view and process to sustainable leadership. Erika takes us on an eloquent journey through leadership - teaching us transformation principles that help us to posture our spirit "BE". King David was said "to have served his generation", the same can be said about Erika McLaurin's epic and pioneers new release, The Be-Attitudes of Leadership.

Shamara D. Cox
Founder | Chief Business Strategist
The Merit Group LLC

Erika McLaurin

INTRODUCTION

In this season, I believe God is looking for leaders who are striving toward kingdom leadership. The Lord spoke to me while sitting at a Joyce Meyer conference, and said "You are going to write a book." He went on to say that I would write a book on the beatitudes, for leaders. He shared that leaders have a greater responsibility when it comes to leading his people. They are not merely teachers but people who are regarded as role models and examples of godliness. As I began to research the topic of leadership, I found the Sermon on the Mount to be very enlightening. This sermon is more than just quotes from Jesus. It is a guide on what kingdom leadership looks like from view point of the Master. Jesus is contrasting the world's view of leadership versus that of the Kingdom views of leadership. The world looks at leadership success from the standpoint of position, money and authority. The Kingdom view of leadership is from the position of being transformed into God's image and likeness. When we look further at the Sermon on the Mount we find:

a. People who were living out the characteristics of the beatitudes were blessed because God has something special for them as a reward. Some rewards were immediate and some were for afterlife in the Kingdom.

b. It showed a direct contrast of the views of life as defined by society.

c. Each beatitude will bring some opposition from society.

d. Jesus showed that he is an example of each beatitude.

e. Each trait challenged the religious leaders and pointed them back to the Old Testament.

As religious leaders, we can become like the religious leaders of the New Testament and lead from a self- righteous view instead of being led by God.   It is my hope that every church leader's goal is to become more like our great leader, Jesus. If so, the Beatitudes for Leaders might and will challenge the way you live in public and in private.

Another interesting thing I found while conducting research on this book was Jesus' audience on that day. Matthew 5:1-2 states "Now when Jesus saw the crowds, he went up on a mountainside and sat down. His disciples came to him, 2 and he began to teach them." (NIV). This passage does not tell us that Jesus began to teach the people but the disciples. The disciples were 12 men (leaders) selected by Jesus who followed and learned at his feet. They were being trained by Jesus to continue spreading the gospel after his death. As we read the Bible, we find that Jesus becomes more and more popular in the people's eyes as he went from town to town healing people. On multiple occasions, we see that the multitude followed him wherever he went. As He became more popular with people, so did his disciples. Jesus knew that if not careful the disciples could find themselves tempted to fall into the trap of feeling important and prideful because they were in Jesus' inner circle. The disciples could find themselves in a level of prestige, where people would be willing to offer positions and money for relationship and association. I believe that Jesus wanted to warn them not to fall into those traps because, as they became more popular, the more people would want to be with them. Instead, he wanted to enlighten them that following him would bring many challenges including opposition and persecution for being a disciple. As Christian leaders, if not careful, we also will find ourselves in a place of popularity and prestige in the eyes of people. This can be spiritually dangerous as a leader because we will find ourselves using the position for personal gain and recognition instead of the true purpose of bringing people into the knowledge of Christ.

In this book, we will look at the Beatitude as a measuring stick for leadership. This is not a self-help manual but rather a thought provoking challenge to review your perception of leadership and may be an opportunity to change your leadership style. I have included personal experiences which will allow you to check your spiritual, emotional and physical leadership thermometer. We will identify four areas for self-examination. In his book, we will explore the symptoms of natural and/or spiritual burnout. Each chapter includes a section of thoughts to ponder. As you reflect on the questions, I encourage you to ponder from a position of where you currently are as opposed to where you want to be. Locate and deal with the authentic you to become a be-attitude leader.

Erika McLaurin

The Cost of Leadership

As we begin to look at the Beatitudes for leaders, we must first look at the definition and qualifications of a leader according to the Bible. A leader is defined as a person who rules, guides, or inspires others[5]. While attending a leadership conference this year, the facilitator asked the audience what their definition of a leader was, and a young lady stated; it is a person who goes against the social norm to lead and inspire people to do what is right. When I think of a leader, I picture someone who is willing to lead by example even when it goes against the grain of the society in which we live in.

In the Church, Jesus is looking for dedicated servants who will lead His people with a good attitude and moral ethics. He is not looking for just anybody to lead, but those who will count the cost of leadership and will accept the responsibility and sacrifices of leadership in the 21st-century church as stated in the following scripture. Luke 14:25-30 states, *"Now great multitudes went with Him. And He turned and said to them, "If anyone comes to Me and does not hate his father and mother, wife and children, brothers and sisters, yes, and his own life also, he cannot be My disciple. And whoever does not bear his cross and come after Me cannot be My disciple. For which of you, intending to build a tower, does not sit down first and count the cost, whether he has enough to finish it lest, after he has laid the foundation, and is not able to finish, all who see it begin to mock him, saying, 'This man began to build and was not able to finish?" (NKJV)* With that in mind, senior leaders should be very careful of who they place in positions of authority. The Bible tells us in 1Thessalonians 5:12a *"and we beseech you, Brethren to know them which labour among you". (KJV)* As a senior leader, we should be looking to see if people meet the requirements of the Bible.

Let's look at the qualifications the Apostle Paul discusses in 1 Timothy 3:1-7 and Titus 1:5-9.

1 Timothy 3: 1-7: "This is a trustworthy saying: "If someone aspires to be an elder, [a] he desires an honorable position." So an elder must be a man whose life is above reproach. He must be faithful to his wife. [b] He must exercise self-control, live wisely, and have a good reputation. He must enjoy having guests in his home, and he must be able to teach. He must not be a heavy drinker[c] or be violent. He must be gentle, not quarrelsome, and not love money. He must manage his own family well, having children who respect and obey him. For if a man cannot manage his own household, how can he take care of God's church? An elder must not be a new believer, because he might become proud, and the devil would cause him to fall.[d] Also, people outside the church must speak well of him so that he will not be disgraced and fall into the devil's trap. (NIV)

Titus 1:6-9 "an elder must live a blameless life. He must be faithful to his wife, [a] and his children must be believers who don't have a reputation for being wild or rebellious. An elder[b] is a manager of God's household, so he must live a blameless life. He must not be arrogant or quick-tempered; he must not be a heavy drinker, [c] violent, or dishonest with money. Rather, he must enjoy having guests in his home, and he must love what is good. He must live wisely and be just. He must live a devout and disciplined life. He must have a strong belief in the trustworthy message he was taught; then he will be able to encourage others with wholesome teaching and show those who oppose it where they are wrong." (NIV)

As we look at1 Timothy 3:1-7 there are several things I would like to point out. The Apostle Paul states: "If someone aspires to be an elder, he desires an honorable position." The first thing I would like us to look at is the word Elder. The word Elder is translated as a leader, pastor, overseer or Bishop depending on the organization he or she represents. The second thing I want us to look at is the part that states: "If some aspire to be an elder." This refers to a person who is interested, desires or feels led to be over a ministry and lead in a particular area of the church. There are times when the Lord calls leaders to a particular position of leadership, and when He does, we need to look at the requirements that go along with the position. I'm a firm believer that whatever God calls us to do, He will equip us.

Ephesians 2:10 "For we are His workmanship, created in Christ Jesus for good works, which God prepared beforehand that we should walk in them." (NKJV) Now, equipping comes in many different forms. You can receive training; attend conferences, read books on how to perform in the position and so on. I have found that, when someone applies for a secular position, they typically research the company in terms of job qualifications and skills needed for the position. This should be the same when you are applying for a church leadership position.

Apostle Paul tells us that it is an honorable thing to desire or aspire to leadership. It is good and honorable to want to be a leader, but at the same time, it comes with strict standards. It is an honor to be called a leader in the house of God. It should be regarded as an honor and not a right. One of the requirements at the church I attend is the leaders faithfully attend weekly Bible study and prayer. For some people that might seem to be an automatic given for leaders. Unfortunately, there seems to be a challenge to get the leaders to participate faithfully. As a leader, we must abide by the standards that have been put in place by senior leadership. If not, we need to examine ourselves to see if we want to be a leader.

The Apostle Paul does not talk much about the skills of a leader but the actual character of a leader. There are many leaders in the church who are very skilled, but that is only part of the requirement of a leader. Leaders should examine themselves to see if they have the character to go along with their skills. An example of this is when someone asks you to give brief remarks during an upcoming service, and you agree. The right thing to do is to be at the service on time and ready to do what you have agreed to do. Instead, they show up late and give remarks beyond the time restrictions. This shows that you might have great oratory skills but your reputation is now tarnished. Another example is when you have been asked to donate your time to paint the church bathrooms. You are a detailed and precise painter by trade, and in the past, you have done a great job. The only problem is no one wants to work with you because you complain about the church asking you to donate your time and you arrive late and yell at the other volunteers. In this example, the painter has great skills, but his personal character erases his/her skills because of their attitude and reputation.

Counting Up the Cost

In both the 1st Timothy and Titus passages, they list several requirements of becoming a leader. I would like to put the requirements into three categories:
* Reputation
* Family
* Life Style

Each of the above categories gives insight into the requirements of good leaders.

Reputation

Good Reputation within the Church
1 Timothy 3:2 "So a church leader must be a man whose life is above reproach. He must be faithful to his wife.[a] He must exercise self-control, live wisely, and have a good reputation." (NLT) A good reputation is how men and women will know you. Your reputation will exceed your life here on earth. I have heard people say on several occasions that they did not care what people thought about them. As a leader in the church, it is vital to have a good reputation among the people. You should have the reputation of being a person of your word, trustworthy and honest. When it comes to people liking you because you are short or tall, attractive or unattractive, etc., then I agree it does not matter what they think. If people are saying they

do not like you because they have found you to be dishonest in your dealings with them, then it is important what they think of you.

Your reputation as a leader in the church can either help to build a solid church or destroy it. I will never forget an instance when my pastor was out of town and left me in charge of the church. One of the ministers came to me and stated that there was going to be an appreciation for one the mothers of our church. This particular mother of the church was very faithful and always willing to help when asked. I explained to him that our pastor had not informed me of the event. He replied that he had talked with the pastor right before he left and apparently, he forgot to tell me. Not wanting to bother the pastor on his trip, I approved the preparation of the dinner. Our pastor returned home from his vacation the following Sunday, just in time for appreciation dinner. Right before the dinner was to begin, I was called into the office by our pastor for clarity on the approval of the dinner. I explained the conversation that I had with the minister and the pastor politely explained that the minister never contacted him before he left and he did not approve the dinner. There are many lessons to be learned from that experience, but the part I want you to take note of is the dishonesty of the other minister. The pastor asked me not to mention our conversation, and he would deal with the other minister. Later I found out from several ministers and members of our church that this particular minister had been found on several occasions to be dishonest. Leaders, dishonesty will cause your reputation to be tarnished.

Good Reputation outside of the Church
1 Timothy 3:7 Also, people outside the church must speak well of him so that he will not be disgraced and fall into the devil's trap. (NLT)

In the section above we discussed the importance of having a good reputation in the church. It is just as important to have a good reputation outside of the church. The majority of the time it is easy to live and act upright when we are at church. The question is, what do people outside of the church think of you? What would your co-worker, whom you see every day, say about you? Or, what would other parents say about you during a child's sporting event or what would the waitress who waited on you after church say about you? As leaders, you must understand that people are always watching you, especially when you have been identified as a Christian. People are watching to see if you will tell the truth when you have made a major error and under great pressure. Will you lie or tell the truth? We can all say, "of course I will tell the truth" when in reality we weigh the consequences that are presently in front of us and make a decision. One day I was at work and was overwhelmed with phone calls. There was one particular customer that complained that I was not returning his calls. I was called into the office and confronted by my supervisor. At that moment, it would have been the customer's word versus mine. I decided, to be honest, and tell my supervisor I was overwhelmed and had not called the customer back but would call him as soon as I got back to my desk. My supervisor explained that we must return calls promptly, but he appreciated me being honest. From that time forward my boss knew that if he asked me something that I would be honest with him despite the consequences.

The passage also states that he would not be disgraced and fall into the devil's trap. It is the enemy's job to stop the progression and growth of the church. Sometimes how we act or treat people outside the church affect how our churches are perceived. While in college I was a shift leader at a popular pizza restaurant in Tulsa,

Oklahoma. I would never forget how much my staff and I would hate to see church folks come in after Friday night and Sunday morning service. I found many of them to be rude and impatient with my staff. Those ministry leaders, worship leaders, and Sunday school teachers would even leave a tract for my staff instead of leaving a tip. This was always disheartening for my staff, and when invited to attend their church, the staff would always decline. The church they attended was known for its great teachings and love, but after experiencing their member's behavior, it discouraged many of my staff from wanting to go visit their church or even receive the salvation of God.

Thoughts to ponder:
1. What will people outside your church say about you and your representation of Christ?
2. Will your actions bring them closer to the Lord or make them not want to be a Christian?

Blameless
   1 Timothy 3: 2 "So a church leader must be a man whose life is above reproach.". (NLT)
Titus 1:6 "An elder must live a blameless life" (NLT)
To be blameless or life without reproach does not mean that you are perfect as a leader but striving to live up to the standard of the Bible. According to Apostle John Tetsola, it is important for leaders to live above reproach. When you are tested, that you are found blameless in the sight of the people you are ministering to. There should not be any question about your lifestyle and walk with God.

Family
   Our first ministry as leaders is to our families. Often we focus

on the church and forget the very ones who are at home. Many marriages have been dissolved due to ministers, leaders, and pastors loving the ministry more than their families. You can say not me, but I ask you to examine yourself. For instance, how many times have you:

- Canceled events with your family to do work for the ministry.
- Heard complaints from your spouse of feeling like a single parent.
- Missed school functions because a church member was in need.

The family is the most important ministry that we have as leaders. There should be a balance between the time you spend with the church, at the church and with solving the problems of your church members. Just as some of us work a 9-5 job and then go home and leave it behind until the next day. That is the same with the ministry. Let's look at what the Apostle Paul says about the family. *1 Timothy 3:4-5 "He must manage his own family well, having children who respect and obey him. For if a man cannot manage his own household, how can he take care of God's church? (NLT) Titus 1:6-7a "6 an elder must live a blameless life. He must be faithful to his wife, [a] and his children must be believers who don't have a reputation for being wild or rebellious. An elder[b] is a manager of God's household,"(NLT)*

Spouse

1 Timothy 3: 2" So an elder must be a man whose life is above reproach. He must be faithful to his wife. (NLT) Titus 1:6-7a "6 an elder must live a blameless life. He must be faithful to his wife, (NLT) Apostle Paul states in this passage that a leader should be faithful to their spouse. They should be faithful to their spouse emotionally, spiritually and physically. When we talk about being faithful, we are to care about their feelings and how our spouses are handling the cares of the ministry. I do understand that there are challenges in ministry that drain a leader. As a result, leaders need an outlet to discuss those challenges with someone. At the same time, their spouses want the same opportunity to discuss the pressures of their lives and to know they are also important. It is great that you are successful in doing your particular ministry, but your spouse wants to know that they have your full attention during dinner or while on a date with you. It is very hurtful to be on a date with your spouse, and they are ignoring you because they are thinking about how they are going to perform a certain project for the church. Also, as a leader, you must be very sensitive to the fact that you are not the only one receiving emotional support from your spouse. Many times, your spouse will desire to discuss their dreams, fears and daily issues on the job with you and have your full attention. When your spouse has an issue, they want to know you are just as much, if not more concerned about how it affects them. They want you to pray with them and give them spiritual insight from the word to encourage them.

There is also the aspect of physical faithfulness. A lot of times we think of being faithful as not committing adultery but there is more to physical faithfulness. Yes, they want you to be intimate with them exclusively, but they also want you to be physically there. For instance, to:

- Have dinner with you.
- Help with the dishes.
- Sit down and watch a movie at the end of the day.
- Be there to help with school projects
- Go to parent-teacher conferences, etc.

Physical intimacy can be reduced when they have had to be a single parent all day, and now you have requested intimacy. Intimacy starts when you get up in the morning and goes throughout the day. It does not start after the kids have gone to bed.

Thoughts to ponder:
1. Are we spending the quality time with your spouse as a couple?
2. When was the last time you talked about something that was not church related?
3. When was the last time you allowed your spouse to share what was on their heart and gave them your full attention?

Children

1 Timothy 3:4-5 "He must manage his own family well, having children who respect and obey him. For if a man cannot manage his own household, how can he take care of God's church? (NLT)
Titus 1:6-7a "6 an elder must live a blameless life. He must be faithful to his wife, [a] and his children must be believers who don't have a reputation for being wild or rebellious. (NLT)
Yes, let's talk about the Children! There are children of leaders who resent their parents being in ministry. When questioned on why they resented their parents and the ministry, they gave hurtful stories of their parents missing sports competitions, recitals and other events that were important to them as a child. Children want time and love from their parents. They wanted to know that their parents supported them but were let down because of their parent's commitment to the ministry. One day while running the School of Ministry for my church, my assistant instructed me to take my daughter home, and she would handle the rest of the night. I declined and asked why she felt that way. She explained that my daughter was there every Monday for three hours while I supervised the classes. Still not

understanding her point, she explained that my daughter looked tired and forgotten. I looked over at my daughter who was asleep with her head resting on the table. I took my assistant's advice. While on the way home, I asked my daughter how she felt about coming and she explained that in the beginning it was cool but three years later, she no longer desired to come every Monday. That day was an eye opener for me. Instead of bringing her on Monday, I would let her visit a friend, and I also worked with my assistant to alternate Mondays. My daughter was excited to be home and able to relax in her room and not at church. Early in ministry, I learned from a great first lady (Yvonne Hubbard) that while raising my daughter I needed to spend time with her, enroll her in activities outside of the church and then go to them. She explained that it is very important to give children a balanced and normal life outside the church. My daughter is 19 years old and is very respectful and loving to the men and women of God. Spending time with her and showing her that she is #1 in my life has helped her to respect my position at the church.

Thoughts to Ponder:
1. When was the last time you took your kids out for a night of fun?
2. How many times have you missed a recital or sporting event to participate in a ministry event?
3. How many Kids have you loved on, while your children were waiting to receive that same love?

Healthy Home
     5 For if a man cannot manage his own household, how can he take care of God's church? (NLT)
If you were going to a financial planner and they seemed to be over their heads in debt, you would not want advice from them. You

would not want to hire a house cleaner and their house was dirty. You wouldn't want to hire a tutor for your child and the tutor did not graduate from high school. Each of the examples listed above are things that we would like the people to be qualified to do. How much more would we expect our leaders to be examples in running a good home?

As leaders we are expected to lead by example and to be an example. Our homes are a representation of how we will lead the ministry. People will be looking at how our spouses treat us and how our children behave. If they do not see love from the spouse, respect from the children and a balanced home, then people will wonder how they can bring love, respect and balance to the church. I remember a minister that I worked with who was having serious marital issues at home. The minister did not have to tell anyone he was having problems at home, his family showed it. He would ask his wife to do something and she would argue with him and tell him to do it himself in front of people. There were times when she would not even come with him to minister at outside churches. His children were even disrespectful to the point that when instructed to do something, they would roll their eyes and ignore him. When asked about stepping back, he declined because he felt the members of the church needed him. I then asked him how you can give counsel to another minister whose family is in the same predicament. What advice would you give them? He was speechless.

Thoughts to ponder?
1. If people looked at your family, what would be their perception of your managing skills?

Life Style

Titus 1:7b-8 He must not be arrogant or quick-tempered; he must not be a heavy drinker, [c] violent, or dishonest with money. Rather, he must enjoy having guests in his home, and he must love what is good. He must live wisely and be just. He must live a devout and disciplined life. (NLT)

According to the Webster dictionary[1] the noun definition for the word lifestyle is the typical way of life of an individual, group or culture. The key phrase of that definition is "typical way of life". As ministers each of us have a typical way of life and it should be a way that is pleasing to God. The Apostle Paul tells us that as leaders "we should not be arrogant or quick- tempered; must not be a heavy drinker, violent or dishonest with money. Instead it is better to enjoy guests, love what is good and live wisely, just, devoted and disciplined life."

As a leader, there is a certain lifestyle that we are expected to live. We should try to steer away from things that would bring destruction or embarrassment to the church. The Apostle Paul gives a list of things that will lead to destruction if not dealt with. An arrogant or prideful spirit will make a person feel more highly of themselves than they really are. If not careful, it can make a person take credit for the things the Lord is doing in their ministry to the point that they no longer lean on God but on their God given gifts and talents. Once they begin leaning on their own gifts and talents they begin to rely on what they know they can do until God has to humble them. A prideful spirit takes away a person's hearing of a direct warning until they fall. The Bible tells us in *Proverb 11:2 "When pride comes, then comes* disgrace, but with the humble is wisdom." (NIV) Proverb 16:18 states "Pride goes before destruction and a haughty spirit before a fall." (NIV) A quick-tempered person is known as a person who loses their temper very quickly. They find themselves not listening but speaking before even thinking. If not careful, this spirit will and can lead to anger or violence. James 1:19b states, "Everyone should be quick to listen, slow to speak and slow to become angry." (NIV) because human anger does not produce the righteousness that God desires. From the passage in Titus, the Apostle Paul gives us three things that will please God. The first is; God wants someone who will love and welcome people into their home and make them feel comfortable. The second thing he wants is leaders who love what is good. This is someone who seeks righteousness and not evil. Their desire is to show His goodness in all that they do by looking at how they can do well towards others. The third way is a how they live.   Leaders are expected to live a wise, just, devoted and disciplined life.

Thoughts to ponder:
1. What does your life style say about you?
2. When was the last time you took the credit for what God did?
3. Do you make people feel comfortable in your home?
4. When was the last time you did something nice for someone?

As we can see as a leader there is a cost that comes with being a leader in the army of the Lord.

"BLESSED"

In the church today there are several words that people have used to the point that the word has lost it value. One word that has been over used is the word Blessed. The word blessed today is translated to being happy. Happy does not capture the true meaning of the word. The term happiness means something happening to someone to bring them joy. Don't get me wrong because happiness does play a part in being blessed but it means so much more. The word blessed means to have an inner joy and peace that comes from being in right standing with God.

Happiness is when you receive a promotion on your job or your son or daughter graduates from school. Blessed is an inner joy that is not determined by if or when you get the promotion. Blessed sees the reward of having a job to support one's, family. Also, your status of being blessed does not change because of the situation, but it is confirmed by an inner divine joy that only comes from the Lord. I always wonder if people feel blessed or if they are just happy. You can see someone on Monday, and they are so blessed because they received a new job, but a few months later they are unhappy because they don't feel they are making enough money. I often want to explain that the blessing is in having the job and not how much money you make. You can have a good job and not feel you make enough, but God ensures that every need is being met in your home. In the beatitudes when Jesus said several times "Blessed are they," He was not only talking about an inner joy and peace but also praise towards their character and a promise of a divine reward.

Let's look at a few scriptures that give us a better idea of being blessed.

God will bless you: *Numbers 6:24-27 "The Lord bless thee and keep thee: The LORD make his face shine upon thee, and be gracious unto thee: The LORD lift up his countenance upon thee, and give thee peace. And they shall put my name upon the children of Israel, and I will bless them." (KJV)*

Walking with God brings a real blessing: *Deuteronomy 11:22-25 "For if ye shall diligently keep all these commandments which I command you, to do them, to love the LORD your God, to walk in all his ways, and to cleave unto him; Then will the LORD drive out all these nations from before you, and ye shall possess greater nations and mightier than yourselves. Every place whereon the soles of your feet shall tread shall be yours: from the wilderness and Lebanon, from the river, the river Euphrates, even unto the uttermost sea shall your coast be. There shall no man be able to stand before you: for the LORD your God shall lay the fear of you and the dread of you upon all the land that ye shall tread upon, as he hath said unto you. (KJV)*

Genesis12:1-2 "The LORD had said to Abram, "Go from your

country, your people and your father's household to the land I will show you." "I will make you into a great nation, and I will bless you; I will make your name great, and you will be a blessing. (KJV)

Empty for God's Use

"Blessed are the poor in spirit: for theirs is the kingdom of heaven."
(Matthew 5:3)

I was shocked to find that the meaning of "poor in spirit" was not correlated to poverty. The meaning of poor in spirit has nothing to do with a person's finances but more of their inner spirit. To be poor in spirit means to be humble or have an emptiness for God to pour into you. Individuals who find themselves living a humble life realize that they have nothing to offer the kingdom of God. They understand that they are entirely dependent on God and acknowledge that without Him they are nothing. These are people who have totally dedicated themselves to the Lord, by humbling themselves and repenting from sin. They have also realized that they can do nothing or be anything without God. There is no arrogance or self-righteousness about them. Being in a place of humbleness frees each person to be used by God.

I found a quote that states "Inner emptiness is a door to God."[2] Each leader will have to empty themselves of their ambitions, desires and the desire to be seen and rewarded by others. For the Lord to use them, they have to be empty so He can fill them with His Spirit, His desires and His plans for their lives. If leaders are full of themselves they will not have room for God to move in their life, as he chooses. There was a time when I planned my life, but God dropped in my spirit to shift and do something different. Since I had my desires, ambitions, and plans, I struggled because of the assignments God had for me did not fit into "my plans".

An example of this was when the Lord instructed me to go back to school. I have always wanted to be an attorney, and I felt this was a very good time to seek my law degree since the Lord was urging me to go back to school. As I sought God's face on which law school to apply to, He informed me that I would not be applying to law school. He was calling me to go back to school to get my master's degree in ministry. I was not happy because that was not what I had in mind when God said I was going back to school. It took a while for me apply. I found myself explaining to God all the reasons I could not go back to school. My excuses included being out of school for an extended period of time. I had not written papers in quite a long time. How am I going to pay for grad school? Lord, I'm not even sure if I could get my transcripts. After all my excuses, the Lord led me to Martin University. Within two weeks I registered for classes, transcripts were ordered, and my financial aid package was complete. Two years later I was promoted to Associate Pastor in my church which required me to apply the knowledge I had gained from my education to my new position. As long as I was trying to map out my destiny, I was prolonging what God had for me. This leads me into the second part of the scripture that states "for theirs are the kingdom of heaven."

When leaders empty themselves to allow the Lord's plans for their lives, they position themselves to receive all that God has promised them. There are gifts and talents that God has preordained for leaders to have. Psalms 139: 16 states, *"Your eyes saw my unformed body; all the days ordained for me were written in your book before one of them came to be." (NIV)*

In other words, before we were born, God mapped out a plan for our lives. God did not just map it out, but He placed it in a book with our name on it. As long as leaders follow the plan of God for their lives, they will inherit every wonderful blessing that He has prepared for them. The more people are willing to humble themselves before the Lord, the more they can receive His fullness. They open themselves to receive His plan, His blessings and most of all His will for their life. Leaders who become more humble in their spirit towards God, they will find themselves becoming more dependent on God. This will open the door for them to do his will here on earth as it is in heaven.

Leaders striving to be kingdom leaders, must continue to stay humble before God. James 4:7-8 gives us a plan of how to stay humble, it states, *"Submit yourselves therefore to God. Resist the devil, and he will flee from you. Draw nigh to God, and he will draw nigh to you. Cleanse your hands, ye sinners; and purify your hearts, ye double minded." (KJV)*

There are four things that he has suggested for us to do: submit ourselves, draw nigh, cleanse our hands and purify our hearts. Let's begin to examine each of these suggestions in more detail.

1. **Submit yourselves therefore to God.** Submit yourself wholly

to the Lord (spirit, soul and body) until there is less of you and more of Him. God wants leaders that are striving to look and act like Him. According to Webster's dictionary, the word submits means, to give over or yield to the power or authority of another. God is asking leaders to yield themselves to His will and plan for them.

2. **Draw nigh to God.** Draw closer to God through prayer and worship. It is imperative to continue to develop an intimate relationship with God. Psalms 27:4 says *"One thing have I desired of the LORD, that will I seek after; that I may dwell in the house of the LORD all the days of my life, to behold the beauty of the LORD, and to enquire in his temple." (KJV)* When leaders desire to come before the Lord, He will not only visit them, but also reveal the mysteries of life. I will never forget what happen to me in 2007. I switched jobs at the leading of the Lord. There was a 30-day lapse between leaving my former job and starting my new job. I decided that I would go to church daily to spend one hour in prayer. I would go into the sanctuary, sit down and just begin talking to God. When I was finished, I felt great but noticed that I had only been praying for 15 minutes. I began to realize that I was only talking at God but not with him as would a friend. The more I went to prayer; the more God began to teach me how to be still and quiet before him. I would come in and start singing songs of worship. Afterwards, I would make my petitions known. Finally, I would sit in silence to hear what God would say to me.

One day in prayer, after I sang to God and made my petitions known, I sat in silence for 15 or 20 minutes. I then heard the Lord say, "Go and purchase a red scarf or covering and tomorrow I am going to visit you." That evening I hurried to get a red scarf because I was so excited that the Lord was going to visit me. I did not know what that was going to look or feel like, but I knew I wanted to be in His presence. The next day I quickly went to prayer so I could worship and then experience the visitation of the Lord. After singing worship songs, I put the scarf on and laid down before the Lord. The minute I laid down, it felt as if someone placed a blanket over me. Immediately the Lord began to talk me. I was in such awe that I could not utter a word. All I could do was listen. God began to explain His plan for that season in my life. He shared with me the areas in my life that He was pleased with and those areas that needed to be surrendered to Him. I have never been the same since that day. I would find myself going to prayer with my red scarf and staying for 1 ½ to 2 hours. I would make lunch dates with friends and find myself praying through lunch. To this day my desire is to lay before the Lord because if I lay in His presence, He will draw near to me. As a leader, it is very hard be prideful when you are constantly in the presence of the Father.

3. **Cleanse your hands.** Spending time with the Lord in prayer conditions you to stay in a place of repentance. David's example of a prayer of repentance can be seen in Psalm 51:1-4 where it states *"Have mercy upon me, O God, according to thy lovingkindness: according to unto the multitude of thy tender mercies blot out my transgressions. Wash me thoroughly from mine iniquity, and cleanse me from my sin. For I acknowledge my transgressions: and my sin is ever before me. Against thee, thee only, have I sinned, and done this evil in thy sight: that thou mightest be justified when thou speakest and be clear when thou judgest."* (KJV) Leaders must understand when they have made a mistake, they cannot hide from God. The minute they begin to hide their mistakes or sin, it eventually leads into other errors or sins and will eventually lead them away from God. It is very hard to lay in the presence of the Lord and to be in sin and hear

from Him. You must first deal with the sin and then from there move forward. Without repentance, leaders can find themselves praying only about things that are important to them. This is when leaders go into prayer and begin to talk about the things that are in their hearts and then get up and leave without hearing what God has to say. They can also stop praying altogether because they are afraid to talk with God about their issues. Leaders must understand that God already knows what they have done and He is waiting to forgive them and bring the relationship back into alignment. I can think of many times that I have sinned and tried to "sweep it under the rug". I would feel that my prayer time was getting shorter and shorter because I did not want to discuss that issue with God. I thank God for His patience! All of a sudden I was not praying as much and my life was getting crazy. I would ask God why is it that my life is so crazy and He would show me an area of sin that I had not repented of. I would quickly repent, and situations would turn around. I will never forget one day while driving, I heard a broadcast by Reverend Kenneth Copeland, and he was talking about the blockage of blessings. Reverend Copeland said "If you feel a blockage in your blessing go back and think of the last thing the Lord told you to do that you did not do. Repent and do the thing God asked you to do." I have found this to be true! The minute I repented and accomplished the task, the blessings began to flow once again.

4. **Purify your heart.** Purify your heart is not just repenting but also turning or releasing anything that stands in the way of your relationship with God. Hebrews 12:1 says *"Wherefore seeing we also are compassed about with so great a cloud of witnesses, let us lay aside every weight and the sin which doth so easily beset us, and let us run with patience the race that is set before us."(KJV)*

Not everything that separates us from God is sin. It could be as simple as sitting on the couch watching television for three to four hours and afterwards being too tired to pray or read the Word of God. I remember a time in my life when the Lord told me I needed to end a relationship that I did not want to end. During that time I found, myself slipping away from the presence of God. I would have one-sided conversations with God knowing that I needed to end the relationship. I missed my time with God, so I ended the relationship and began to pray again, but it was not the same. On my way to work one day, I was talking to God, He stopped me and said: "You are angry with me." I was silent because I had grown up believing I couldn't tell God I was angry with him. Again the Lord said "Admit it, you are angry with me. I already know you're mad." All of the sudden I burst into tears and said "Yes, I am angry. I don't know why I had to end the relationship." The Lord said," I did it out of love for you". I repented for my behavior, and the Lord began to minister to my hurt and pain. He didn't owe me an explanation, but he explained things to me that were hidden while I was in the relationship. Oh, how I love God!

Thoughts to ponder:
1. What has God asked you to give up and you have refused?
2. What hidden anger have you not revealed to the Lord?
3. Spend time in worship and ask the Lord to reveal any areas that he would like to empty in your life...in your ministry...in your relationships.

Erika McLaurin

GRIEVED FOR CHANGE

"Blessed are they that mourn: for they shall be comforted."
(Matthew 5:4)

As we look at the verse above, we can clearly think of the loss of a person or thing. Blessed are those that mourn means so much more depending on your perspective. I urge you to think out of the box as a leader as you read this chapter. The Webster Dictionary(1) gives two different definitions for the word mourn. The first definition is, to feel or show great sadness because someone has died. Typically when we hear the word mourn, we think of death, and that would be correct. We all mourn when a friend or loved one dies, and the grief can be unbearable. We will find ourselves going through a roller coaster of emotions such as denial and isolation, anger, bargaining, depression and finally acceptance.

The second definition of the word mourn is to feel or show great sadness or unhappiness about something. I want to explore that great sadness about that "something" in this chapter. While reading the book "7 Signpost to Your Assignment" by Mike Murdock,[3]

-43-

something captured my attention. He talked about understanding your calling. I have spoken to so many people who have explained that they are searching for what God has called them to do while on earth. Every leader was created to solve a problem in the land. The question is, what problem were you created to solve? In the search to find what you were called to do, you can relate to some of the same feelings you get when you are mourning the loss of someone. In various training sessions, I have asked leaders, what makes them cry because whatever makes you cry will give you a very good idea of what you were called to do. When ministers expressed how grieved they are about the senseless loss of young people, I have found them to be some of the greatest youth leaders. Some have said they grieve over the mistreatment of the elderly and they find themselves working with seniors. Often leaders have made it complicated while pondering the question of who am I and why was I created. When leaders are "lost" and looking for that assignment, they sometimes find themselves in assignments that were never meant for them. I can recall an instance before I became a minister; I was at a small church and searching for what God wanted me to do. I was an usher, but that did not fill the void within me. I then joined the choir, and for someone who is tone death, I quickly found out with the help of the choir director that singing in the choir was not my Gift. I will never forget going to a visiting church, and the choir director told me she could hear my voice over everyone else. I was so excited because I thought she was saying I did a great job, but only to find out that I was singing louder and more out of tune than everyone else. As you can see that was not my calling in life. I then began to teach a Sunday school class for the youth and all of a sudden I felt like I was making a difference. The void was starting to close in on my search. As time went on, I accepted my calling into the ministry, and it seemed as though God would move upon me when I would minister. I remember one day, going to work very disgruntled about my job and asking God when He was going to release me from this job. I graduated from college to be a broadcaster and not an insurance adjuster. I clearly heard the Lord say to me that I was a broadcaster, I paused because I thought the Lord had not noticed I was clearly working for an insurance company. I heard him say in my spirit, "I called you to broadcast the good news of Jesus". This was my confirmation, and from this point I began to move forward in my calling.

Once I found that my calling was to minister, the question was, to what age group and populations. Part one was finding my calling, and part two was to finding my assignment. I have taught all age groups, from children to adults. I have also taught new believers to the most mature believers. In 2007, I enrolled in the New Wineskin Ministries International School of Ministry and was ordained. At my former church, the pastor did a lot of hands-on training of ministers and I thought that was the procedure for all churches. However, as I matured in the Word of God and met other ministers, I discovered that it was not the same procedure in every church. A large number of ministers had accepted their calling and were waiting to read a scripture on Sunday. I would ask them if they witnessed in the community, worked at the altar, conducted devotion or visited the sick and shut-ins. They would look at me perplexed. I would ask them if they had been trained in those areas at their church and the answer was no. I inquired whether they had been taught to prepare a sermon and deliver it. Their answer was no. Many were waiting for the day they would preach their first sermon, but they had not been trained. My heart was broken. How can we license a minster and not give them the tools to succeed in ministry? I was grieved and from this I knew what my assignment was in the Kingdom. I was called to the assignment of training ministers and leaders for the Kingdom. I applied for the position of Director of the School of Ministry and was placed there. I prayed to God for the right classes to offer to ministers which would equip them for the ministry that lay ahead. God granted my request, as of present, I have been the director for seven years. I will not say that once you find your assignment that it will be easy because that is when the fight begins. When I first received the position, not everyone was happy, but I was okay with that. There was much work to be done, and I was up for the challenge.

When you have found the right assignment you will get excited about what you are doing. The void is being filled because you have yielded to God's plan for your life and things are coming into alignment. There are times when I get very frustrated and tired while in my assignment but on the student's graduation day, I feel fulfilled at the accomplishments of the students.

In conclusion, another way to look at the beatitude of this chapter is, "Blessed are those who grieve for their assignment in life and are comforted when they come into alignment with their destiny".

Thoughts to Ponder:
1. What grieves you? Abuse? Poverty? Sickness? Abortion? Alcoholism? Drug abuse? Battered women? Abandonment? Lack of education?
2. What measures will you take to stop the grieving in that area?

Humility Out Weighs Pride

"Blessed are the meek: for they shall inherit the earth."
(Matthew 5:5)

According to the world's point of view meekness can be seen as a disadvantage for a leader, but in reality, it is one of the most powerful advantage a good leader can have. When you think of meekness people fall into two categories, that of being humble or prideful. They will either develop the character of being humble or prideful. Every leader makes daily decisions that impact their career. You can choose to be humble and satisfied with taking a back seat and serving someone else's vision until you are promoted by God or you can be prideful and serve only yourself. Humble leaders do not mind serving someone else's vision until God promotes them.

The word humble means not proud or haughty and not arrogant or assertive. To be the leader God has called you to be, you must be humble. In Luke 14:7-11 Jesus tells a parable about being humble and taking the lower place, it says *"So He told a parable to those who were invited, when He noted how they chose the best places, saying to them: When you are invited by anyone to a wedding feast, do not sit down in the best place, lest one more honorable than you be invited by him; and he who invited you and him come and say to you, 'Give place to this man,' and then you begin with shame to take the lowest place. But when you are invited, go and sit down in the lowest place, so that when he who invited you comes he may say to you, 'Friend, go up higher.' Then you will have glory in the presence of those who sit at the table with you. For whoever exalts himself will be humbled, and he who humbles himself will be exalted." (NKJV)* In this parable, Jesus speaks about going to a wedding, sitting in the best seat and being asked to move so that someone more important can have your seat. Jesus suggests that we take a lower seat and be asked to come to a more elevated one. I and many friends in ministry have experienced this type of embarrassment. I will never forget being invited to an ordination service by a sister church. When my friend and I arrived, the church was crowded, and the seating was very limited. At the time of the incident I was the associate pastor at my church and the director of our school of ministry. I just knew I was deserving of being seated up front next to the Bishop of my church. The usher explained that there were two seats in the back. I aggressively but sweetly requested that we be seated up front next to the bishop. The usher led me and my friend to the front row. As we were getting ready to sit down, the bishop informed me that the seat I wanted was the mistress of ceremony's seat and I would have to sit elsewhere. As you might guess, I had to go back to the usher who found us seats on the very end of the row. I was so embarrassed but I learned my lesson. What we should have done was take the back seats and wait to be asked to move to the front. I took my position as associate pastor and director of the school of ministry as reason to be recognized and seated on the front row. An attitude of meekness is what I should have modeled instead of the prideful attitude I had. Another aspect of being a humble leader is having a servant's heart. A leader with a servant's heart, is one who can honor, listen, and follow directions of their current leaders even when there are challenges. We can find in the Bible two good examples of leaders with a servant's heart through Joshua and David.

There are a lot of great examples in the Bible that show the benefits of how good mentoring between a mentor and the mentee can empower and prepare the mentee for the assignment ahead of them. One example of this is Moses and Joshua: Numbers 27:15-23 states, *"Moses said to the LORD, "May the LORD, the God who gives breath to all living things, appoint someone over this community to go out and come in before them, one who will lead them out and bring them in, so the LORD's people will not be like sheep without a shepherd." So the LORD said to Moses, "Take Joshua son of Nun, a man in whom is the spirit of leadership, [a] and lay your hand on him. Have him stand before Eleazar the priest and the entire assembly and commission him in their presence. Give him some of your authority, so the whole Israelite community will obey him. He is to stand before Eleazar the priest, who will obtain decisions for him by inquiring of the Urim before the LORD. At his command, he and the entire community of the Israelites will go out, and at his command, they will come in." Moses did as the LORD commanded him. He took Joshua and had him stand before Eleazar the priest and the whole assembly. Then he laid his hands on him and commissioned him, as the LORD instructed through Moses." (NIV)*

Just imagine having to lead in the place of someone who was a great leader. Joshua was Moses' assistant and learned firsthand what it meant to lead God's people. We are not talking about leading a few hundred but millions of people. Moses taught Joshua how to love, care for and most of all lead a challenging and stubborn people. It was because of his one-on-one training by Moses that allowed him to lead the Israelites into the Promised Land. It is pertinent that leaders partner themselves with a "Moses" who will not only teach them how to fulfill their assignment but also be a great role model. Leaders must be followers who are teachable and humble under the leadership in which they serve. Apostle John Tetsola in his book, "The Anointing of the Second Best" stated that an assistant can be anointed, educated and skilled under their designated leader but they are not the one God has chosen to be the senior leader at that time. [4] Likewise, if the assistant embraces the teachings of their mentor, they will not only help the mentor go to the next level, but they too will move to the next level.

I can point to two men who have mentored me to become the minister and leader that I am today. The first man is Pastor Donald Hubbard. When I was called to the ministry Pastor Hubbard took me under his wing and taught me how to be a minister. He showed me how to write sermons, understand pulpit etiquette, and how to love people where they are. I can remember a woman at our church who would yell at her children from the choir stand. I would get so upset with Pastor Hubbard because he would never reprimand the lady for yelling at her children. One day I asked him why he would not say anything to the woman about her behavior. He said, "Minister Erika, we must allow the wheat and tares to grow together and the Lord will separate". Unfortunately, his explanation did not answer my question. One Sunday he was out of town, and left me in charge of the morning service. While I was in his office, this lady knocked on the door and asked if she could come in. At first, I wanted to say no, but the Holy Spirit urged me to let her in. When she came in, she apologized for her behavior and explained that she was overwhelmed having to raise her sister's two children and her granddaughter. She was an older lady and had raised her children. She explained it was like starting over again much like a single mom. Consequently, when she got to church on Sunday she would be on edge. This edginess is why she yelled at the children when they acted up. For the first time, I saw her as a hurting woman. From that day forward I began to pray for her and help her with the children when they came to church. When Pastor Hubbard returned, I explained what happened, and he explained that we could not judge the situation from our eyes but the eyes of God. That day I learned what it meant to put things and people in God's hands and let Him deal with them in His own way.

The other man who has mentored me is my current Pastor Mark Brown. Pastor Brown has mentored me in the administration side of the ministry. There have been times when he has taken me aside after a team meeting and asked if I understood why we made a particular decision. Sometimes I understood and other times I felt the outcome should have been different. In the latter case, he would explain that when we make decisions we have to consider the ministry as a whole and how the decision affects the body versus one particular ministry. Since working under Pastor Brown, I have learned to listen to people's requests and pray over them to ascertain what God is saying. There are times when the team's ideas have been great. However, I have to stop and consider their relevance and timing for our church. The role models of Pastors Hubbard and Brown have taught me how to love people and how to efficiently run a ministry.

Unfortunately, not every leader has a great mentor and the mentee relationship. Some leaders have had to work under challenging circumstances but through perseverance they have become great leaders. We can look at the relationship between David and Saul. This is very different relationship compared to the relationship of Joshua and Moses. David shows us how to be a humble servant leader under challenging circumstances.

1 Samuel 17:55-58 and 18:5-9 says, *"As Saul watched David going out to meet the Philistine, he said to Abner, commander of the army, "Abner, whose son is that young man?" Abner replied, "As surely as you live, Your Majesty, I don't know." The king said, "Find out whose son this young man is." As soon as David returned from killing the Philistine, Abner took him and brought him before Saul, with David still holding the Philistine's head. "Whose, son are you, young man?" Saul asked him. David said, "I am the son of your servant Jesse of Bethlehem." (NIV)*

1 Samuel 18: 5-9 states *"Whatever mission Saul sent him on, David was so successful that Saul gave him a high rank in the army. This pleased all the troops, and Saul's officers as well. When the men were returning home after David had killed the Philistine, the women came out from all the towns of Israel to meet King Saul with singing and dancing, with joyful songs and with timbrels and lyres. As they danced, they sang: "Saul has slain his thousands, and David his tens of thousands." Saul was very angry; this refrain displeased him greatly. "They have credited David with tens of thousand," he thought, "but me with only thousands. What more can he get but the kingdom?" And from that time on Saul kept a close eye on David. (NIV)*

The first passage above presents to us the beginning relationship between David and Saul that was favorable. The second passage presents to us the change in the relationship. We see that as David was coming back from a war with the Philistines, Saul inquired about the young warrior. He wanted to know who he was and where he came from. I believe Saul saw great potential in David and wanted to groom him for more significant victories. According to the passage, every battle that Saul sent David on was very successful. So successful that David rose to one of the high-ranking positions in the army. We must understand that while David was rising, he faced challenges from his leader.

Saul was happy with the success of David and their victories war until he became jealous. David was coming from a victorious battle and the people praised him more than Saul. This is the change or shift that took place in the relationship. Now the protégé is being praised over the mentor. Unfortunately, not every leader can handle others receiving more praise than themselves. David is a perfect example of how to continue to serve while the person training you is trying to destroy you. I have also served under a challenging leader. This particular leader would verbally degrade me in front of the team when I would make suggestions that the team thought were good. At the end of our programs she would introduce the team and not mention me until the team said something. She would take my ideas as her own and then take the credit. I would ask her about it and she would state "I made some changes, so it was actually my idea". This was very hurtful to experience by the person who is supposed to be mentoring you. Friends in the ministry would advise me to report the verbal degrading to my bishop. I would pray about reporting it to my bishop but the Lord would tell me His grace is sufficient. This was very hard but I continue to serve under her humbly. As I continued to work underneath her with a servant heart, God continued to give me favor in other areas of leadership. I will never forget the day that my bishop asked me to serve as a Council of Elders. In order to take the position, I would have to leave the team. This was a bitter sweet moment. I was sad to leave my team members but happy to be released from my leader. When I told the team they were very excited for me but not my leader. As expected, she degrade me and my position to the team. I just stood there and thanked God in my mind.

As we can see both Joshua and David had servant's hearts and did great things when the mantle was passed on to them.

Thought to ponder:
1. How will you work under a challenging leader?

STARVING FOR MORE

"Blessed are those who hunger and thirst for righteousness, for they will be filled." (Matthew 5:6)

The Psalmist states in Psalm 42: 1-2 *"As the deer pants for streams of water, so my soul pants for you, my God. My soul thirsts for God, for the living God. When can I go and meet with God? (NIV)* When we look at the beatitudes on the blessing for those being hungry and thirsty, we think about a person being malnourished. The word malnourished means to be poorly or improperly nourished; suffering from malnutrition. Leaders can be malnourished physically from not eating the right things. They can also become spiritually malnourished when they fill their lives with their personal agendas, schedules, meetings, and commitments that prohibit spending time with God. It can result in us operating in our strength and not the strength of God.

I can remember hearing a story of a preacher who was conducting a 40-day revival in the name of Jesus. He would get up early in the morning to say a small prayer and go out to preach. At night he would come in and lie down and say another short prayer thanking God. By the 21st day, the man said to God, Lord I am so tired and don't know what to minister tonight. The Lord responded, so are you ready to hear what I want to minister on this evening? The man quickly repented and began to pray. That night he had the greatest outpouring of the Holy Spirit with people coming to Christ, being healed and families being reunited. The man was so busy trying to do the work of the ministry that he forgot to consult the one he was ministering for. In the world we live in everything is instant gratification. We are either on our I-phones, I-pads, or computers trying to fit all the demands of leadership into one day. As a result, we are exhausted by the time we go to bed. This chapter will allow us to look at what it means to be malnourished from the lack of time before the Lord and the consequences of spiritual burnout that affects the leader and the people they lead.

For leaders to understand the significance of being malnourished and the effects of being burned out from malnutrition. The phrase spiritual burnout is described as the daily pressures of ministry that leaves a leader feeling tired and worn out. Most leaders find themselves always teaching, mentoring and taking care of the needs of the people without taking the time to take care of themselves spiritually.

There are four types of burnout that a leader can experience. A leader can experience physical, relational, emotional or spiritual burn out.[2]

A physical burnout results from a lack of exercise, unhealthy eating, stress, and lack of sleep due to overworking and worrying. It is your body's way of saying I cannot continue to function in this condition. I found that when I pushed myself to continue working, even when I was exhausted, my body would shut down and I had no choice but to rest.

A relational burnout is the result of working with other leaders or people who drain all the energy from you after you are finished working with them. Every leader that has been in leadership a long time has experienced a person who continually comes to you for an extended period of time for advice but never takes the advice. Another example is a person that continues to complain to you about all the things that are wrong but never has a solution. You may have come to church or a meeting in a great mood but after your conversation with them, you are emotionally drained. I know that does not happen at your church or place of business, just mine. Ok, I need you to stop right here and repent right now!

An emotional burnout happens when a leader feels he/she has no one to go to during the difficult times. They continue to pour out but there is no one to pour back into them. Some leaders actually feel a sense of loneliness because there is no one they feel safe talking to.

The last type of burnout is a spiritual burn out. Spiritual burnout is a result of leaders neglecting their spiritual lives while they take care of other people's spiritual needs. There is a drain that happens when leaders do not stop to refresh and refuel their spirit by spending quality time with God. Leaders must understand that there is a difference between spending quality time with God and the quantity of time they spend with God. If you as a leader are in a place where you no longer desire to read the Bible or find praying a chore, then you are at the point of spiritual burnout. All too often by the time a leader realizes that they are spiritually burned out, it is too late. They no longer really want to continue in ministry or have anything to do with it. I have seen great leaders leave the ministry because they were tired and no longer found joy in the church. I can relate to a time in my ministry where I was so busy with projects that Sundays were more of a work day for me and not an actual day of worship. On one particular Sunday, we were having a ministry fair after morning service. During the service I was unable to concentrate on the word of God because I was so busy thinking of all the things that needed to be done. My focus was on the setup of the fair and wondering if the ministers were prepared to encourage the people to take advantage of their ministries. Also wanting the pastor to be pleased with the results. It was at that moment that God began to speak to me that I was operating like Martha in Luke 10:38-42 and very little like Mary. I was convicted because I had to stop and think of all the times I was working on projects during Bible study, the morning worship and prayer on Thursday that I no longer took the time to just sit in his presence and worship him. Often I would find myself praying quick prayers in the morning and at night. I would talk to God during the day but never take the time to allow God to speak back to me. I was becoming irritated with people when they did not keep their promises. I was disappointed when things did not work out the way I expected them to. I even found myself operating out of my flesh saying and doing things that no longer was part of my Christian character. There was an instance one day when I was so angry because people were not working as hard as I felt they should be working on projects and before I knew it I said a curse word. I was so shocked that that word came out of my mouth! When I gave my life to the Lord I gave up cursing so the mere fact that I was so angry that I cursed allowed me to see that I had become empty in the word, in prayer and in my relationship with Christ. It was then that I knew I needed a change. So I repented before God and asked God to give me a renewed desire for him and the word. It was not easy but I had to take the time to step back and reevaluate my priorities. I had to intentionally begin to pray, to read my Bible and most of all spend more intimate time with Christ.

During this time I read a book by Wayne Cordero called "Leading on Empty." This book taught me that you must stop and refuel.[1] There are some suggestions to help you refuel your spirit and bring back your joy for ministry.

1. **Self-evaluations** of where you are is very vital. You must look at the things that drain your energy and the things that refresh you.
     The things that can drain you are:
    a. Long meetings
    b. Having repetitive conversations about the same thing
    c. A lack of commitment to promises people make.
    d. Overpromising my time to please people.
     The things that can refresh you:
    a. Prayer
    b. Reading books
    c. Cooking
    d. Spending time with your family
I had to begin to decrease the things that drain me and do more of the things that refreshed my mind and my spirit.

2. **Set time aside to pray and to read the word.** Psalms 1:2-3 *"but whose delight is in the law of the Lord, and who meditates on his*

Erika McLaurin

law day and night. That person is like a tree planted by streams of water, which yields its fruit in season and whose leaf does not wither whatever they do prospers." (NIV) When leaders begin to take the time to read the word, to pray and to listen to God allows them to re-create a love for Him and the word. This will allow them to grow and flourish in due season.

3. **Take a vacation.** There are times when leaders need to step away from their church or ministry duties and responsibilities to regroup. Previously, I requested a few weeks off to just spend time with God. This was tough for me at first because my mind wanted to focus on my projects, but my spirit wanted to relax. I thank God for good friends and a staff that held me accountable while on vacation. While on vacation I received phone calls with questions and as hard as it was, I had to redirect people to my staff. I must admit after the first week it was refreshing not to have to worry about things at the church. I felt at peace. I was able to have quality time with God to read the word because I desired to read the word. I began to pray for one hour each day and allow God to refill me. I felt stronger during that vacation in the Lord. It felt great to be able to focus on the things that God had promised me but most of all I was able to see that I was tired because I took projects that were not assigned to me by God. During that time of prayer, I began to ask God where we as leaders went wrong. I explained to the Lord that there were so many leaders who were tired and worn out that wanted to give up their assignments in the ministry. The Lord clearly spoke to me and said it seemed that my leaders are doing things in their strength and not mine. They are taking on projects without ever consulting me. In other words, they were doing assignments in their strength instead of seeking God continuously during the process to get new revelation

and strength.

Leaders must focus on spending more time learning about God and not so much time trying to work for God. If you allow God to refresh and refuel you when you are low, it will enable you to avoid the many different types of burnout.

Thoughts to ponder:
1. Are there things in your life that could contribute to you being malnutrition?
2. What steps will you take to prevent physical, relational, emotional and spiritual burnout?

LEAD BY FORIVENESS

"Blessed are the Merciful for they shall receive Mercy."
(Matthew 5:7)

As I look at the word "mercy," the definition of the word means a kind or forgiving attitude towards somebody that you have the power to harm or right to punish. (Oxford dictionary)(6) One word in the definition I would like to consider is the word "forgiveness." As a leader, there will always be ups and downs. You will find as a leader that people will betray you intentionally and non-intentionally. They sometimes do not follow instructions because they believe that they are more intelligent and have better knowledge than you. Yes, this sometimes can create hurt feelings for you as the leader. This is the very reason we have to count up the cost when we sign up for a leadership position. The key is to forgive them before it settles in your heart. I know it is easier said than done but a leader must lead by example through their actions. There are two aspects I would like to look at in this chapter about forgiveness. I want to examine the visible aspect of forgiveness which is to forgive those who have hurt you as a leader. The other aspect I will look at is forgiving yourself for the mistakes that you have made as a leader.

Forgiving Others

I know as leaders we are typically told to forgive others for their wrongdoing, and this is true. It is important to understand that everyone makes mistakes, even us. I want to do a play on the word "lead." In this portion of the chapter, I want to use the word as following by forgiveness. Matthew 6:14-15 clearly states *"For if you forgive men their trespasses, your heavenly Father will also forgive you. But if you do not forgive men their trespasses, neither will your Father forgive your trespasses. (NKJV)* The desire to be forgiven by God should cause leaders to forgive the people who have betrayed them. If the leader chooses not to forgive, then they are positioning themselves not to be forgiven by God. I can think back to a time in ministry when I had a very skilled and anointed assistant; she was always ready to do whatever was needed for any project that I asked her to work on. She came with great ideas and a passion for each project. So one particular season she introduced a great ministry idea. I thought it was well planned and very practical but explained that I would have to present this to the senior pastor. After discussing the project with the senior pastor, he felt it was a very good idea but this was not the right time for the ministry. He did agree, however, that this would be something that we can do in the near future. My assistant became quite upset and began to withdraw from the church. I was unaware that she decided to leave the church, so I called and called her with no response. I was very concerned that something might have happened to her. I didn't know if she was sick or working additional hours at her job. I just knew something was wrong. I even asked our church secretary to reach out to her, and again my assistant would not respond. I continued to try to contact her for six months with the hope that she would reach back out to me. Finally, while talking to one of our members about my concerns about my assistant not contacting me; they shared that my assistant had become offended because we had not honored her request for the project. My assistant felt that as hard as she worked for the church, her request should have been honored. I was taken back that a lady I had worked with for two years left the church because her request was not honored. I must be honest, I was furious with her because she was so offended that she decided to not only walk away from the ministries that she was currently leading but ultimately the church. As a leader, I found myself being angry at her for several weeks. Every time I thought about the situation I became even more furious. Now, of course, the correct thing would have been to pray for her, but I wasn't there yet. I felt betrayed by someone I thought I knew very well, but in reality, I didn't know her at all. Finally, the Lord dealt with me about the unforgiveness in my heart, and I tried to explain to him that her reason for quitting was petty and the Holy Spirit allowed me to see that my reason for unforgiveness was petty. When the Holy Spirit allow me to see that my justification for not forgiving her was invalid, I then turned to God and asked for forgiveness. I asked God to forgive me for not forgiving her. Then I had to forgive her in my heart and pray for her. As a leader, it is never our desire that someone that we work with is hurt and offended. The lady did return to our church for a short season. When she first came back I realized that I had not fully forgiven her. I know this because when I saw her, I became upset all over again. I had to go back to God and forgive her again. I was not going to allow the enemy to have rule over my heart because I would not forgive. The next time I saw the lady; I embraced her and told her how much I had missed her smiling face at the church. She was genuinely surprised by my actions, and I felt a complete release of love towards her.

Now that is just one of my stories, but yours might be that they didn't show up for a meeting, they didn't do their part of the project, maybe they complained the whole time while doing the project. In the midst of that, you have become angry with him/her to the point of unforgiveness. No matter what it is, it is not enough to give room to the enemy in your heart. When we choose not to forgive people, we open the door to be tormented by demonic spirits. We can find an example of this in Matthew 18:23-35 it states, *"Therefore the kingdom of heaven is like a certain king who wanted to settle accounts with his servants. And when he had begun to settle accounts, one was brought to him who owed him ten thousand talents. But as he was not able to pay, his master commanded that he be sold, with his wife and children and all that he had, and that payment be made. The servant therefore fell down before him, saying, 'Master, have patience with me, and I will pay you all.' Then the master of that servant was moved with compassion, released him, and forgave him the debt. "But that servant went out and found one of his fellow servants who owed him a hundred denarii; and he laid hands on him and took him by the throat, saying, 'Pay me what you owe!' So his fellow servant fell down at his feet[a] and begged him, saying, 'Have patience with me, and I will pay you all.'[b] And he would not, but went and threw him into prison till he should pay the debt. So when his fellow servants saw what had been done, they were very grieved, and came and told their master all that had been done. Then his master, after he had called him, said to him, 'You wicked servant! I forgave you all that debt because you begged me. Should you not also have had compassion on your fellow servant, just as I had pity on you?' And his master was angry, and delivered him to the torturers until he should pay all that was due to him. "So My heavenly Father also will do to you if each of you, from his heart, does not forgive his brother his trespasses." (NKJV)*

As we can see in verse 34 and 35 that the master delivered the man into the hands of his tormentors until his debt was paid all because he would not forgive the debt of someone else. Likewise, our heavenly Father will also do the same if each of the leaders does not forgive your brother. What does this mean? This means you will be open to allowing the enemy to continue to play the same issue over and over until bitterness sets in. Once bitterness has set in, it will lead to anger. So when you see the person your thoughts go to I don't like them, they're untrustworthy, I don't care if they are sick or lose their job because bitterness and anger have plucked out all levels of compassion for that person. If not careful that bitterness will make a leader gossip or talk very bad about the person to others. In the beginning, the leader will feel justified for sharing what happened, but this can lead to character assassination by the leader. This can also put other leaders on defense. Some leaders might feel "I do not want to be on the wrong side of leader M" or if I mess up will they talk about me the way they're talking about that person. It is never good for people to fear what will happen to them if they make a mistake. As leaders, you want people to know that if they make a mistake, it is okay. Also, if you have to correct them, they know you are correcting them in love.

Let me share a few tips for forgiveness:
1. **Verbally say you have forgiven them.** You might not feel like you forgave them, but forgiveness is an action and not a feeling. An

example is: I forgive Margaret for yelling at me in front of the training class.

2. **Write it down and throw it away.** This will allow you to express what happened and how it made you feel.

3. **Confront them about what happened.** Matthew 18:15 states, *"Moreover if thy brother shall trespass against thee, go and tell him his fault between thee and him alone: if he shall hear thee, thou hast gained thy brother." (KJV)*

4. **Look at it from the other person's perspective.** There are times when we only see it from our perspective. Was there something we said or did that led to the person's actions or statement? Did we say something that offended them in advance? We must look at both sides.

5. *R*ealize you've made mistakes and needed forgiveness.** So forgive them as you have been forgiven.

Let's stop and say a quick prayer:

Lord God I humbly come before you thanking you for your loving kindness and forgiveness of my sins. As you have forgiven me I would like to forgive _____. I ask that you release any hurt, anger or bitterness from my heart that I hold against _____. Lord, I ask that you will bless them and their family. I pray that you would bless them on their job and in their finances. I come against sickness in their body I pray blessings over them, and I ask that you will fill them with your love, peace, and joy. Thank you, Lord, for releasing me from the hurt and pain that arose from the incident. I love you, Lord.

Forgiving Yourself

As we have talked about giving others, there is one more person that we need to forgive and that person is you. As a leader, you will make mistakes, make wrong decisions and sometimes say the wrong thing to someone because you are human. As you travel this journey of leadership, you are going to make mistakes, but you have to learn to forgive yourself. If you do not forgive yourself, you can find yourself not moving forward because you are allowing those mistakes to define you and it can leave you spiritual blinded to the promises of God.

God has created each of us to solve some problem in the world, and if the enemy can get leaders stuck on their past mistakes, then they will not move forward in the things that God has for them. In 1 John 1:9 it states, *"If we (**Leaders**) confess our sins (**tell God what you did. Not why you did it but what you did**), He (**God**) is faithful and just and will forgive us (**God is faithful to forgive us. God is not like man who might or might not forgive us, He is true to his word.**) of all (**God is faithful to forgive us of all, not some, of our wrong doing.**) our sins and purify (**cleanse our heart and mind**) us from all unrighteousness (**evil doing and thoughts**)."* (NIV) God's word has given leaders a promise that he will forgive them when they ask. For most leaders it is not hard to believe and accept the scripture. The hard part is moving forward with the forgiveness that is given in that scripture. The enemy wants leaders to feel as if they have to do something extra to get God to forgive you. Here's what some leaders do; they say Lord forgive me for speaking harshly to my assistant. I did not mean to say it in the way that I did; please forgive me, Lord. At that time God forgives them, yet two days later they are still dwelling on how harshly they spoke to their assistant. They have asked their assistant for forgiveness, they have asked God for forgiveness, and both have forgiven them, but they tend to not forgive themselves. This also happens when leaders have sought advice from their team but chooses not to take the advice. Unfortunately, the decision that they made was not the best decision, and now they are embarrassed. The leader has asked the team to forgive them for the mistake that they made. Again, the people have forgiven them, but they cannot forgive themselves. When a leader is in this position, they find themselves struggling to make other decisions that affect their church or team. They begin second-guessing themselves on the simplest things because they are now afraid to make a decision, or they chose to not make a decision at all. They feel that the team has lost faith in them because they made a wrong decision. This is farthest from the truth; it is more frustrating for the team because they are looking for the leader to lead them. The goal is to learn from your mistake and move forward. Understand leaders, the enemy also wants to make you doubt yourself when new problems arise. But remember in every decision that we make we must seek God and ask Him to lead and guide us.

When leaders have not forgiven themselves, they find themselves putting on blinders that will hinder their spiritual vision. The unforgiveness will begin to make them make decisions out of the eyes of guilt, hurt and shame. If not careful, you can become very negative and judgmental because you are carrying unforgiveness in your heart. This will position them to make inaccurate assessments on projects and about people. This particular type of blinder will not allow the leader to see the future from the eyes of God. It will hinder them from making decisions with confidence. If they are unable to see things from a place of forgiveness, they obstruct the growth in their lives and their team. God has a plan for each leader and has called leaders to develop the people being led by them. It is very hard to see the great plan God has for you if you feel that everything you do is wrong and question how God can use someone like me. God sees the greatness in you and wants you to see that greatness as well. God knew you were going to make mistakes and still opened new doors of opportunity. This is when leaders learn from the mistake and accept the grace and mercy that has been granted. God is not looking to punish you but to pick you up and walk with you.

Let's stop and say a quick prayer:

Dear Lord, I thank you for your grace and mercy. I thank you that your word is true and that I can confess my sins and you will forgive me. I now ask you to help me to forgive myself for my sins. Allow me to release my past mistakes and help me to move forward in the future that you have planned for me. I come against spiritual blindness, and I ask that you will bless me that I will make good and conscious decisions out of the eyes of love and forgiveness. Lord, I choose today to see myself and the greatness that you have placed in me from your eyes. Thank you, Lord, for forgiving me and loving me only as you can. I thank you and Love you, Lord. Amen.

I believe that forgiveness is so important for those in leadership. As we can see, if leaders plan to walk in the great things of God they must take the time to clear their hearts by forgiving people but most of all by forgiving themselves.

Thoughts to ponder:
1. Are there people you need to forgive?
2. What mistake have you made that you have not forgiven yourself for?

THE REAL DEAL
BECOMING AUTHENTIC

"Blessed are the pure in heart, for they will see God."
(Matthew 5:8)

When we look at the phrase "pure in heart" in the scripture it refers to someone who is sincere, honest and without hypocrisy. Sincere when dealing with others and with themselves. Take an honest assessment of your strengths and weaknesses. Are you comfortable in being your unique you? Have you discovere and used the gifts that God placed in you for your calling and ministry? Are you operating from a place of total reliance on God and allowing God to operate through you? As a leader, it can become very easy to imitate someone whom you have found to be very successful in what they do. They can find it simpler to mimic someone then try to find out who they are. I can remember early in ministry my pastor asked several of us to participate in teaching Bible study. Each one of us was given a topic and scripture from which we were to teach. I was excited but nervous because I started to compare myself to the other two teachers. There were some significant differences between them and myself. The first difference was I tend to be a very practical living teacher, whereas giving examples that relate to everyday life. My counterparts were more focused on knowledge based information than everyday living. Another difference was that, I like to free flow teach from an outline and my counterparts loved to teach using a PowerPoint. So for this assignment I decided I was going to be like my counterparts and teach from PowerPoint using lots of scriptures. I figured if they can do it, then so could I. WRONG! When it came to my night to teach, I abandoned my outline, practical teaching style and prepared the PowerPoint. I must admit this did not go well for me. I found myself struggling to follow the PowerPoint, and the people in the class looked confused. In the middle of my teaching, I just stopped and stated, "This is not working for me". I turned the PowerPoint off and took out my outline. It was then that I felt the anointing of the Holy Spirit. It was such a powerful experience. I was able to flow freely and teach on a practical level. The problem for many leaders is, they want to imitate other successful leaders. I was reading a quote by an unnamed leader, and it said: "To wish you were someone else is to waste the person you are." This speaks volumes. To wish or desire to be someone else other than who God created me to be is like throwing away the person (dreams, gifts, and talents) that I was created to be. Psalms 139:14 states *"I will praise thee; for I am fearfully and wonderfully made: marvellous are thy works; and that my soul knoweth right well."(KJV)* God created each leader to be unique in what they do. My area of leadership was tailor-made for me by God. As I began to prepare to launch my leadership training company, I had to research other leaders who had been successful in leadership training. So as I was researching the most powerful leadership trainers in America, I found that each one of them specializes in a particular area of leadership. Yes, they were very knowledgeable in other areas of leadership but found the specific area they were to specialize in. Once they found their field, they positioned themselves to become experts in that area of leadership training. These successful leaders wrote books, magazine articles and traveled the world teaching seminars focused on their area of expertise.

One way to become successful as a leader is to find out what area of leadership God has called you to operate in. If God has called you to be a youth leader, you need to seek God to find out what area you are to lead within the youth department. It can become very overwhelming when you feel you were called to the youth department and you are working as the craft leader, the worship leader, the outreach leader and an event coordinator. The question is; which area has God gifted you to work in within the youth department? Yes, I believe that you can be called to be a youth leader but I believe God wants you to specialize in that one area he is drawing you to work in and perfect it. I can remember the day I was installed as the associate pastor at my church. I was the first associate pastor under our current senior pastor. When I took on the position, I found myself being extremely busy and exhausted because I was the Operations Pastor, the Congregational care pastor, and the assistant to the pastor. I also worked a full-time job and was a single mother raising two daughters. After two years, our senior pastor created a Pastoral team in which each of us was given a particular area of ministry. My new official role or position was Pastor of Operations. Once I was given my particular area on the pastoral team, I began to research what my job duties were and started to work in that area.

God has created a special area for every leader where they can be the leader who fulfills the plan God has for their life. You can only do that by walking in the plan that was set for you. Trying to be someone else will not allow you to accomplish the plan God has for you. It will not allow you to do a fraction of what you were created for. If we look at Psalms 139: 16 states, *"Thine eyes did see my substance, yet being unperfect; and in thy book all my members were written, which in continuance were fashioned, when as yet there was none of them.". (KJV)* There was a book that was written about you before you were even born. I don't know about you, but I don't want to get to heaven and find out I only completed part of my assignment because I was trying to be like someone else. Another way of looking at this is to think of all the people who are waiting on you to be you. They are waiting for you to accomplish the assignments that have been given to you. It has taken me three years to write this book. In the midst of writing it, I asked God why certain doors He promised would be opened had not opened yet. God's response was "Where are you on the book because there are people waiting on this book?" After that, I felt compelled to write again. To confirm what God had said to me, I let one of my very close friends read the first three chapters of this book and every time she saw me she would say, "Where is the rest of the book?" I would explain to her that I was working on it, but I had other things that I needed to finish. Her response was, "I need you to hurry up and complete the book because leaders need this in their lives." As time went on, she became my accountability partner and would always remind me that I needed to set aside some time to complete the book. Her words were a reminder of the question God asked me every time I questioned Him about doors being opened for me.

It's not enough to just be a leader but you must be an authentic leader. An authentic leader is someone who is determined to know the plan of God for their life and is willing to walk in that designed plan. This goes back to being pure in heart with who God has called you to be. I cannot stress enough, that if a leader tries to be someone he/she is not, they will never accomplish the plan or reach the people they are destined to lead.

I declare and decree that those reading this book will become the authentic leaders God has called them to be. I declare and decree that they will complete the assignments that have been given to them by God. By doing so, they shall reach every person they have been assigned to reach.

Thoughts to Ponder:
1. What is the last instruction that the Lord has given that you haven't followed through on?
2. Ask the Lord to show you any areas that you are operating in a less than authentic manner?

The Atmosphere Changer

"Blessed are the peacemakers, for they will be called children of God." (Matthew 5:9)

Leaders have been called to be peace makers and atmosphere changers. They are called to be the people who make a difference in the lives of people and their community. Matthews 5:13 say, *"Ye are the salt of the earth: but if the salt have lost his savour, wherewith shall it be salted? it is thenceforth good for nothing, but to be cast out, and to be trodden under foot of men". (KJV)* Salt is an ingredient that changes the flavor of things. It can make something that is bland become very tasteful. Salt does a multitude of things, but for this chapter, let's look at the seasoning and preservative qualities of salt.

Salt as Seasoning

Let's look at salt as a seasoning. Have you ever been to a family member's house for dinner and when you bite into the food there is no salt? The first thing you do is ask for the salt to season the dish. So, as a leader it is our job to season the lives of people who feel that they have no hope. It's your job as a leader to add something to their lives that enhances their lives. You must evaluate; am I creating a positive and welcoming environment when I meet with my team? Is there constant pressure and uneasiness present? When you deposit a life changing seasoning into people's lives, they are changed for the better. A few years ago, we were doing some leadership training, and the topic was; "How to Build a Strong Staff Relationship." While attending the training, I didn't feel that I treated my team badly but what I realized was that I was not taking the time to speak into their lives. After that class, I decided to take each of them out individually to get to know them and begin to pray for them and the concerns in their lives. Not just that day, but I try to send encouraging messages to them to keep them uplifted. Within weeks I began to see a different working relationship because I was taking the time to pray for them and to speak into their lives. I found myself caring about the things that they cared about. I would pray for their children, their finances, their health and most of all their relationship with the Father.

Now salt can also be very harmful to the body. Too much salt can create things such as high blood pressure. The wrong salt amongst leaders can create high blood pressure. Any time we as leaders find ourselves not caring about the need of our team or putting high demands on them, we can set an atmosphere of negativity. This is when your staff only comes to a meeting out of obligation and not because they want to be there. An example is when the leader comes in and does not ask how everyone is doing but goes right into their agenda. Another example is when a leader comes into a meeting, and they want to discuss all the things that went wrong without giving credit for the things that went well. For some people, this works well, but for the average team member, this is mentally and spiritually draining. They find themselves leaving the meeting feeling defeated and powerless. If not careful they will begin to treat their staff the same way they were treated. Remember it is the leader's responsibility to enhance and empower the life of their team.

Salt as a Preservative

Another thing salt is good for is preserving things. Salt helps to prolong freshness making food safe for a longer period. According to the Webster Dictionary, the word "preserve" means to keep alive or in existence. Leaders are called to preserve the lives of people by being an example of how to handle difficult situations. It is their job to keep hope alive within people. You might ask how can I keep a person alive? You keep them alive by speaking words of encouragement to the people you encounter. It could be as simple as giving them a compliment on their smile or telling them what a good job they are doing on a project. Some people are dying from stress, discouragement, and depression. As leaders, we should have enough of the word of God in us to share with individuals who feel they have no hope. Jesus is the Hope of life and the giver of joy. John 10:10b states *"I have come that they may have life and that they may have it more abundantly." (NKJV)* Jesus came to preserve the lives of people who have no hope. I know this to be true. I have been in stores and noticed that someone was having a bad day and after a kind word and a compliment I have seen their face light up. Why? There are times when people need someone to speak words of affirmation to them.

In the second part of the passage Matthew 5:14-16 it states *"You are the light of the world. A town built on a hill cannot be hidden. Neither do people light a lamp and put it under a bowl. Instead they put it on its stand, and it gives light to everyone in the house. In the same way, let your light shine before others, that they may see your good deeds and glorify your Father in heaven".* *(NIV)* It is key that we examine the importance of being a light of the world. This passage takes us back to the theme "Carriers of the kingdom". So, when you step into a place where there is strife and negativity, as a kingdom carrier you bring the light of peace and positivity. A leader should be able to walk into a place and people recognized that there is something different about them. I tell people all the time that you do not have to wear a cross or carry a Bible in public for people to know that you are different. It is how you carry yourself because of your relationship with the Father. It is your demeanor that says you love God. At my current job, I started out working as an order entry temporary worker. Before I took this assignment, I was working in the ministry full-time but needed to go back to work to earn extra income to pay some additional expenses for my daughter graduation. I was not happy about leaving full-time ministry to go back to work, but I had a daughter getting ready to go to college. I felt I was stepping out of the will of God to make provision for myself. I accepted the position as order entry temporary worker with the understanding that I would be there only four weeks and then return to full-time ministry. God had a different plan for me. When I first got to the company I was very antisocial because I knew I would only be there for a limited time. When they asked me to pick a desk I chose a desk on the other side of the room. I did not feel since I was only going to be working there for a short time that I should make friends. Every day I went to work it was a struggle because I did not want to be there. I remember one day talking to one of my friends and saying how much I did not want to be there and she said ask God what the assignment is for you at that company and do it. When I asked what my assignment was I realized it was to be a light to the women in that department. God works in funny ways, because when I came to grips I was reassigned a new seat in the heart of my department. Once there I got to know my co-worker. I didn't necessarily talk about God with my coworker but the way I conduct myself made a difference. I try to do things right not wrong. Even when I made a mistake and was questioned about it I was very honest, owning my errors. This was very impressive to some of the ladies because they felt it would be easier for me to have lied than told the truth. I explained to them no matter how bad the situation gets it is better to be honest and to face the consequences than to be known as a liar. There were days when God would reveal to me certain things about people that I only knew through His revelation and knowledge. One day my coworker shared with me a difficult situation in her life and she later told me that she loved the fact that we worked in the same area. She said, "there is something about you that makes me feel good and peaceful". I wanted to shout that it is the Holy Spirit in me resting in this place.

We had a speaker in our area and each person would get a chance to pick a radio station. I would never choose a station and one of the girls asked what station I would like to listen to. I declined because I did not want to stir up any issues by bringing Christ into the workplace. She asked again and I told her I listen to K-Love which is a Christian radio station. She proceeded to turn on K-Love and put it on the speaker. At first I was very nervous about a song that came on about the blood of Jesus. However, it did not create a problem among the other workers. After several weeks, my coworker would tune into K-Love and she began asking questions about God. In that same period, several Christians asked about starting a Bible study and we did. We took prayer requests and watched God fulfil those requests. I could see the atmosphere in my department changing and lives being changed because I was willing to be obedient to the assignment God had given me in this place.

One of the people that God allowed me to speak into their life was my boss at that time. I'll never forget that day. He was having a rough day and he said, "Ms. Erika can I have a hug?" At first I was a little leery because of sexual harassment laws but I felt a release from God to do so. When he hugged me, he hugged me tight and I could feel the weight of life dropping off him. From that day forward I received favor from him. As my assignment was ending my boss came to me and shared that the order entry position was closing but he had another position to offer me. He asked if I would be willing to be cross-trained in his department and I said yes. Over the last two years I have been able to speak into different people's lives on my job.

I hope this chapter motivated and explained that you have more influence in the lives of people than you realized. Understand that everywhere you go you are representing God. Just as salt is used to change the flavor of food so are leaders called to change the atmosphere of an environment.

Thoughts to Ponder:
1. As a leader, are you changing the atmosphere where you are?
2. Are people saying that there is something different about you?
3. Do you fit in with everyone else?

4. Is your light shining in private (family and friends) and public (the workplace) where the Father God can be glorified? If not, I ask you to go back and examine why your light is not shining bright and make a conscious decision to be the light that will bring glory to God.

.

#

"Blessed are they which are persecuted for righteousness' sake: for theirs is the kingdom of heaven." (Matthew 5:10)

Today we live in a society where people see wrong as right and right as wrong. We live in a society that expects leaders to lie, not keep their promises and do unethical things with no consequences. I have seen politicians lie and when confronted by their supporters, they explain that it is okay because all politician lie about what they are going to do. This should not be the norm. I just imagine doing the right thing and getting in trouble for it. A situation comes up at work and you are asked it you had any involvement in it. You could lie and shift the blame to someone else or tell the truth and face the consequences. Telling the truth could result in a write-up or termination. The choice is yours, to tell the truth, or conveniently lie. As a Christian leader, you are held to a different standard and level of accountability. These standards are outlined in the word of God. The Bible teaches honesty and fair practices in business.

When I think of the civil rights movement, I think of how Martin

Luther King took a stand against the injustices being done to African Americans. He took on the norms of society to improve the lives of all American and eventually lost his life in the process. Today we can see the many benefits of his sacrifices being displayed in society.

Each leader needs to know who they are, what they stand for and who they stand for. Once a leader has established those three facts it will shape how they make decisions that concern their businesses, their team members, and their ministries.

As a godly leader, you need to know who you are in Christ. You are a born-again Christian who was made in the image of God. You are no longer your own but an ambassador for God.

2 Corinthians 5:20 states, *"We are therefore Christ's ambassadors, as though God were making his appeal through us. We implore you on Christ's behalf: Be reconciled to God As an ambassador for God, you act on his behalf"*. (NIV) To represent Christ, you must know and have the heart of Christ. When you think of foreign ambassadors, they are given the authority to act on behalf of their country. No one questions what they represent and what authority they have when making statements and decisions on behalf of their country. As an ambassador, people may never see the leader of your country, but you stand in the name of that leader. As Christian ambassadors, people should know who you represent. They should know that you have the authority and full backing of God when you make decisions on behalf of God. You must think from a Kingdom mindset before making decisions. There was a time when people would use the phrase "What Would Jesus Do?" As a leader, you will need to ask that same question. How would Jesus handle

the situation? What would Jesus response be to the people involved in the situation? It is critical that we ask these questions and proceed with the heart and the mind of Christ.

As a leader, you must stand for righteous living? Do you believe that you could tell a little white lie and it doesn't matter? Do you think it's okay to borrow money from the business without permission? Is it okay to cheat on your spouse or abuse your children? The answer to each of these questions should be a resounding NO. Some would say, "I would never do any of those things. I remember my position as a young minister when I was and still working for an insurance company. One day I was asked to do something I felt was unethical and I declined to do it. My boss put me on the spot knowing I was a Christian. He asked if this was a moral issue for me. I boldly expressed to him that I could not and would not do it because it went against my beliefs. My counterparts were very shocked by my response, and my boss was embarrassed. From that day forward my boss made it very hard for me to work in peace. He had my files pulled for audit. He would give me unreasonable deadlines and carefully monitor my time. This was a time of much prayer on my face before God. I could have done what he asked and destroyed my witness among my co-workers who knew I was a Christian. Despite the unknown consequences, I chose to obey God rather than my boss. That decision helped to pave the way for me to stand for righteous in my everyday life. It is very easy to stand for righteousness when there is nothing to your detriment, but when your job is on the line it is a different matter. Will you choose to do what is right, or do what is convenient? As a leader, you must do what is right and leave the consequences up to God. When I left the company, my boss expressed his respect for me and wished me the best at my next company. As a result, I could go back to that company if I chose to and get my job back. Knowing what you stand for will help you to gain favor with people. You must believe in honesty and ethical living because you represent the Father.

Leaders must understand that when you know who you are in Christ and choose to stand for what is right, there will always be some form of opposition. The opposition may be great but not unbearable. As you stand with and for God, He will stand with you. Again, there is going to be opposition, but we should be able to stand for what we believe in and through that people will be drawn to the God we serve.

Thoughts to Ponder:
1. Do you know who you are in Christ?
2. Are you willing to take a stand, even it cost you?

POSITIONED FOR OPPOSITION

*"Blessed are ye, when men shall revile you, and persecute you,
and shall say all manner of evil against you falsely, for my sake."*
(Matthew 5:11)

In the previous chapter, we talked about standing for righteousness despite what the outcome may be. We discussed understanding that you are what you stand for and who you stand for. In this chapter, we will talk about standing strong on the word and the promises of God for your business, health, team, company or ministry. There are times that God will give you a vision for your ministry, your business, your life, etc. and people will disagree with that vision. When leaders tell me that people do not agree with their vision, I ask them "What did God say to you?" If God said it, then you have to be willing to stand on it until it comes to pass. We can look at several examples in the Bible of men who had to stand on the promise of the Word of God despite what it looked like. We can look at Moses and how he led the people through the Red Sea. I'm sure when God told Moses to go through the Red Sea there was some doubt, but he knew if God said it, then God was going to make a way for them to go across the Red Sea.

Joshua is another example. God clearly told him that "I am with you and I'll never leave you nor forsake you". He also told him to not look at the faces of the people. He successfully led them into the promise land.

Gideon is also another example of a man given a tough assignment. To fulfill his assignment, he was told to decrease his army with the understanding that his army was already small in comparison to that of his enemies. But Gideon decided to trust God and was victorious.

I am sure in each one of these situations there were those who complained, disagreed and possibly felt they had a better plan than the leader in charge. As a leader, you must not be moved by people who disagree with you about God's assignment. Your job is to lead people and not be led by them. I have talked with several leaders who have aborted the vision God gave them because the pressure of the people was so great. An excellent example of a leader who faced considerable opposition was Nehemiah. Nehemiah was truly a great leader. He faced all sorts of obstacles as he was rebuilding the walls of Jerusalem. He was maligned, as well as threatened, but he did not give up. He finished rebuilding the wall with God's help and protection.

I can remember when I was installed as associate pastor. The morning of the installation I was lying in bed and questioning God concerning the position. I was excited for the opportunity but nervous because I was only 34 years-old and would be helping to lead 300 - 400 members. As I talked with God about my fears, the Lord dropped in my spirit that they did not choose me, but He did. From that word alone I took a deep breath and said, "okay God I trust you". That very word was tested over and over my first year in the position. I had people tell me that I asked for the position and that I wasn't qualified for it. There were times when I had people who would not take my word and would go to the senior pastor to verify it; only to be told that the issue had been approved by him. I even had someone say to me that I was not the associate pastor and that was only a title given to me. They said they would never call me their pastor. All of this occurred during my first year in the position. The opposition was not just from people within my church, but I also had opposition from family members. Several family members expressed their concern about me taking the position as an associate pastor while being a single mom, working a full-time job and being able to perform all of them efficiently. In my strength, I could not, but I had to stand on the word that God gave me, God said to me, "I have given you this position, not man". In that year, there were times I cried out to God and asked, "Why am I in this position?" The Holy Spirit would remind me that I was in this position for a reason, and despite how I was treated I was on assignment. It is now seven years later, and I can say that God has been faithful to me because I did not quit. I must admit there were several times that I wanted to turn in my keys and my title and not serve any longer but each time I wanted to quit, the Lord would bring back to my memory His word of, "I placed you in this position." He would remind me He was walking right alongside me and if I trusted him I would be victorious in every situation. The same people who questioned my position and went over my head now tell me how happy they are with me as the associate pastor, and how they appreciate all that I do to help them in the ministry. I could not give up my position because of people. God called me to the position, and I was and am yet determined to fulfill my assignment as Pastor of Operations.

Leaders have said to me that they're not sure they could have gone through what I went through, and my response is always, if God has told you that he assigned you to a position, then he will give you the grace to complete the assignment if you stand on his word.

As a leader, it is your job to walk in the promise and assignment that God has given you for your life and not fear people. Do not be afraid of what people think about your vision. Always remember the vision God gave you and be encouraged that He will lead you every step of the way. Opposition in any leadership position will make you stronger if you allow it to be so. You must learn not to take the comments or actions of people personally. Look back and recall how God has helped you to trust His word over people's opinions.

You must remember that you are on assignment and people are watching to see how you react in various circumstances.

Thought to Ponder:
1. What has God told you to do that is on hold because people have said or done things against you?

I'T's WORTH THE COST

"Rejoice, and be exceeding glad: for great is your reward in heaven:
for so persecuted they the prophets which were before you"
(Matthew 5:12)

Rejoice because as you walk out your assignment God is with you. As I mentioned earlier in chapter four of this book, each of you were created to solve a problem here on Earth. Sometimes when we first begin the journey, we have a hard time trying to figure out all the pieces of the puzzle. The more we humble ourselves in the presence of God, the more we see the pieces coming together in our lives. When I started in the ministry 16 years ago, I would never have thought I would be writing a book on the attitudes of leaders. I thought my journey and experience was crazy, but now I am grateful for the journey. I can see how the experiences I have had in leadership were precursors to my training others to be leaders. The experiences you have will make you an excellent example of what God can do in the lives of others when you choose to have the attitudes of the Kingdom. It is amazing to watch the transformation of leaders from the mindset of "I think I may be called to be a leader" to that of knowing they are called to be a leader. Not just called, but willing to be trained and taught how to handle the issues that arise in serving as a leader.

Let's look at a few biblical leaders who accepted the challenge.
1. Abraham: He believed God when he told him he would be the father of many nations although he was older and supposedly unable to have children. God honored his faith and gave him Isaac. We as Christians are now living in that fulfillment.
2. Moses: Led the people out of bondage although they murmured, complained and came against him. He stuck with the plan of God in the wilderness in the face of opposition.
3. Joshua: God had to continue to remind and encourage him that he was with him through the journey and he led the people into the promise land.
4. Paul: After his conversion to Christ, Paul stopped persecuting the church. He became the Apostle to the Gentiles. He established many churches, trained young pastors and wrote much of the New Testament even through his persecution.
5. Jesus: Jesus is our greatest example of what a leader should be. He came from heaven, putting all things aside to walk the earth and to die that each of us would have access to the Father.

Each of the above leaders faced opposition but accepted the assignment given to them following God's leading in the process. There were times when they got discouraged. The difference was they did not let this keep them from seeing the greater picture of what was at stake. Do not get stuck in your circumstances because the reward is greater than the sacrifice.
Thought to Ponder:

1. Are you willing to be challenged and to remain steadfast in the assignment of leadership God has entrusted to you?

BIBLIOGRAPHY

[1] Coderio, Wayne, "Leading on Empty: Refilling Your Tank and Renewing Your Passion" Bethany House, 2010

[2] Halloran, Kevin (2013, October). Christian Ministry Burnout: Preventions, Signs, Statistics, and Recovery. Retrieved from http://www.leadershipresources.org/blog/ christian-ministry-burnout-prevention-signs-statistics-recovery/

[3] Murdock, Mike, "Finding Your Purpose in Life" The Wisdom Center,2001

[4] Tetsola, John, "The Anointing of the Seconds Best" New York: Burback ,2010

[5] Merriam- Webster Dictionary, https://www.merriam-webster.com/

THE BLESSING PRAYER

Dear Lord,

I pray that every leader who has read this book understands that there is a cost to leadership.

I pray that as they humble themselves in your presence, they will search for the assignment that you are calling them to do.

I pray they will desire even more of you and your presence.

I pray that their eyes and hearts are open to forgiving those who have hurt them and to forgive themselves for their mistakes. I thank you, Lord, that you are a God of love and forgiveness.

I pray that each leader will become what you have called them to become. Lord, I pray that their ears will be close to the words and voices of people and open to your voice and your voice only.

I pray they will be atmosphere changers everywhere they go. As they teach, mentor and conduct Kingdom businesses and that Your anointing will cover them. Allow them to walk in such a way that Your presence in them shifts the atmosphere from darkness to light.

I pray that the decisions they make will be according to the leading of the Holy Spirit.

I pray they will not be offended by people who disagree or do not understand their calling.

I pray they will come to know who they are, what they believe and who stands with them when opposition comes their way.

I pray they will stand firm on the promises that you have made to them despite what they see.

I thank you, Lord, for each leader and I pray that the plan you have for their lives will be fulfilled. I charge them to press towards the higher calling which is in You and refuse to allow the enemy to derail them.

I declare and decree:

Increase in their businesses and their ministry.

Increase in their finances and resources.

Favor and open doors of opportunity.

Favor with God and man.

Increased desire and strength to fulfill the purpose you have ordained for their lives.

That you Lord will receive all the Glory.

In Jesus name, Amen.

ABOUT THE AUTHOR

Pastor Erika is the founder and president of the McLaurin Center for Emerging Leadership since 2015. She has worked for eight years as an Operational Manager for New Wineskin Ministries, where she serves on the advisory board, finance council, as well as oversees the organizational leaders. In this role, she has developed a leadership training module, and an integral part of the redevelopment of the ministerial procedures, protocol. In addition, she has served for eight years as the Director of the New Wineskin Ministries International School of Ministry where she is responsible for establishing relevant curriculum for ministers.

Erika holds the following accolades an M.A., in Urban Ministry from Martin University; an M.S., in Pastoral Care and Counseling from Southern Theological Institute of Biblical Studies; a B.A., in Communications from Oral Roberts University; Associate Degree in Insurance from the Insurance Institute of America; a Certificate of Ordination from New Wineskin School of Ministry, and a Certificate in Radio and Television from the Gary Area Career Center.

Erika currently lives in Indianapolis with her two daughters.

BOOKS COMING FALL 2018

THE SECRET OF THE PULPIT
Depression and Burnout Among Pastors

This book will explore what burnout and depression is, how it affects pastors and what can be done to prevent it. It will also review scripture to explore a foundational, theoretical perspective regarding burnout and depression that challenges pastors in the 21st century.

COFFEE WITH THE MASTER
A 31-Day Devotion for Leaders on the Go

For most leaders the morning begins with a hot cup of coffee to get the day going. This book will give leaders a daily spiritual cup of coffee and the necessary boost to make it through the day with God.

84175574R00059

Made in the USA
Lexington, KY
21 March 2018